ISBN 978-1-998317-64-6

Cover illustration and design by Charlotte Chang with the aid of artificial intelligence.

First Edition: January, 2025

一千三百多年前，在古老的中国唐朝，

一个武姓开国功臣家里出生了一个小女孩。

那时候，人们很少记录女孩的名字，

所以她的名字已经无人知晓。

Over 1,300 years ago, in ancient China during the Tang Dynasty, a baby girl was born into a wealthy family with the last name Wu.

Back then, people didn't usually write down girls' first names, so no one remembers what hers was.

武家的父母非常重视学习，希望她能变得有学问、有才华。那时，大多数女孩没有像男孩那样的读书机会，但她学会了音律、写字和读书，还懂得如何做出明智的判断。渐渐地，她变得才华出众，聪慧过人。

Wu's parents thought learning was important. They wanted Wu to study many things, even though most girls didn't go to school like boys did at the time. Wu learned music, writing, reading, history, and how to make smart decisions. She became very clever.

4

14岁时，她被选入太宗皇帝的宫中，成为众多妃子之一。宫里有许多女子，但她凭借聪明才智和勤奋努力脱颖而出。

When Wu was 14 years old, she went to live in the palace of Emperor Taizong as one of his concubines.

There were many women in the palace, but Wu stood out because of her clever ideas and hard work.

tài zōng huáng dì qù shì hòu, tā hé qí tā méi yǒu hái zǐ de fēi zǐ yī
太宗皇帝去世后，她和其他没有孩子的妃子一
yàng, bèi sòng dào sì miào chū jiā wéi ní。 tā de gōng tíng shēng huó sì hū
样，被送到寺庙出家为尼。她的宫廷生活似乎
jiù cǐ jié shù, dàn tā de gù shì yuǎn méi yǒu huà shàng jù hào
就此结束，但她的故事远没有画上句号。

When Emperor Taizong passed away, Wu, like the
other concubines without children, was sent to a
Buddhist temple to become a nun.
It seemed her life at the palace was over—but
Wu's story wasn't finished yet.

8

几年以后，太宗的儿子高宗皇帝将她接回了皇宫。高宗非常器重她的才智和见识。不久后，她深受宠爱，晋升为皇后。

Years later, Emperor Gaozong, the son of Emperor Taizong, brought Wu back to the palace.
She married him, and he admired her for her sharp mind and wise advice.
Soon, Wu became his favorite and rose to the position of empress.

成为皇后后，她协助丈夫治理国家。
高宗皇帝生病时，她接管了许多政务，
做出了许多重要决策，证明了自己是一个强大
又有智慧的领导者。

As Empress, Wu helped her husband run China.
When Emperor Gaozong became sick, she took
over many of his duties.
Wu made big decisions and showed that she was a
strong and capable leader.

12

公元690年，她决定成为皇帝——中国的最高统治者。她是中国历史上第一位也是唯一一位女皇帝。她的尊号"则天"，意思是"效法上天"。她建立了周朝，并以智慧治理国家。

In 690 CE, Wu decided to become emperor— the ruler of all China. She was the first and only woman in Chinese history to do this. Wu took a new name, "Zetian," which means "Model of Heaven." She started a new dynasty called Zhou and ruled wisely.

13

14

作为皇帝，她任用人才时注重能力，而不是家世背景。她还帮助农民种出更多粮食，并大力支持教育和艺术。

在她的统治下，唐朝变得富裕而强大。

As Emperor, Wu picked people to help her based on their skills, not their family background.
She also helped farmers grow more food and supported education and the arts.
Under her rule, China became rich and strong.

她为自己的名字选择了一个全新的汉字："曌"，意思是"日月凌空，普照大地"。她希望用这个字来表达自己要成为人们的光明和指引。

Wu chose a brand new Chinese character for her first name: "曌 (zhao)."It means "shining like the sun and moon."
She wanted to be a bright and guiding light for her people.

18

有些人认为女人不能成为好皇帝，但她用行动
证明了他们错了。在她的领导下，唐朝变得更
加强大。贸易、文化和艺术都繁荣起来。

Some people didn't think a woman could be a good
emperor, but Wu proved them wrong.
Under her leadership, China grew stronger.
Trade, culture, and art all flourished.

公元705年，81岁的她去世了。

她留下了一座特别的碑，叫做"无字碑"。

碑上没有刻字，她要让人们自己决定如何记住她。

When Wu passed away in 705 CE at the age of 81, she left behind a special monument called the "Wordless Stele."

It had no words on it, so people could decide for themselves how to remember her.

今天，武则天被人们记作一位睿智而无畏的领袖，她改变了历史的进程。

她的故事告诉我们，只要有勇气、努力和决心，任何人都能成就伟大。

Today, Wu Zetian is remembered as a brilliant and fearless leader who changed history.
Her story shows us that anyone can achieve greatness with courage, hard work, and determination.

24

www.ingramcontent.com/pod-product-compliance
Lightning Source LLC
Chambersburg PA
CBHW041450120626
46547CB00002B/397